Helping Children See Jesus

ISBN: 978-1-64104-045-7

SATAN AND HIS DEMONS
New Testament Volume 8: Life of Christ Part 8

Author: Ruth B. Greiner
Illustrator: Frances H. Hertzler
Colorization courtesy of Good Life Ministries
Typesetting and Layout: Morgan Melton, Patricia Pope

© 2018 Bible Visuals International
PO Box 153, Akron, PA 17501-0153
Phone: (717) 859-1131
www.biblevisuals.org

All rights reserved. No part of this publication may be reproduced, stored in a retrieval system or transmitted in any form by any means, electronic, mechanical, photocopy, recording or otherwise, without the prior permission of the publisher, except as provided by USA copyright law.

RELATED ITEMS

To access related items (such as activities, memory verse posters and translated texts) please visit our web store at www.biblevisuals.org and enter 1008 at the top right of the web page. You may need to reduce the zoom setting to get the search box.

FREE TEXT DOWNLOAD

To obtain a FREE printable copy of the English teaching text (PDF format) under Product Format, please scroll down and select Extra–PDF Teacher Text Download. Then under Language select English before clicking the ADD TO CART button to place in your shopping cart. Other languages are available at an additional cost from the Language menu. When checking out, use coupon code XTACSV17 at checkout and click on Apply Coupon to receive the discount on the English text.

Submit yourselves therefore to God. Resist the devil, and he will flee from you. — James 4:7

Lesson 1
A MAN DELIVERED FROM DEMONS

NOTE TO THE TEACHER

It is important for Christians to know something about Satan and his demons.

Satan, the "god of this world" (2 Corinthians 4:4) and the "prince of the power of the air" (Ephesians 2:2), is a mighty foe. His purposes are to defeat the plan of God and to promote his own kingdom. He has a well-organized army of demons to help carry out his evil plans. Demons are wise, intelligent, evil spirits who serve their leader, Satan.

The first lesson in this volume teaches something of the character of demons. Although demons know many things which humans may not know, they are not all-knowing nor nearly as wise as God and His perfect Son, the Lord Jesus Christ. This fact should encourage the believer in Christ.

You are continually reaching out for the lost. Therefore, you doubtless have in your class those who have not been born again. All unbelievers are open to demon possession. (See Ephesians 2:2.)

This series of lessons should help each one to understand that no matter how vile the sinner, the Lord Jesus Christ is willing and able to cleanse him, forgive him, and give him a clean, new heart. (See Psalm 51:2, 5; Ezekiel 36:26.) Satan and his demons may be stronger, wiser, and more cunning than we are. But Jesus Christ is Victor over Satan and all his hosts.

The word "legion" in the lesson means a vast number. In the Roman army, a legion was as many as 6,000 soldiers. You may wish to explain this to your students.

Scripture to be studied: Mark 5:1-21; Luke 8:26-40; Matthew 8:28-34

The *aim* of the lesson: To teach that although demons may be stronger than we are, Jesus Christ is Victor over them.

What your students should *know*: Jesus has greater power than all the demons.

What your students should *feel*: An awareness of the power of demons.

What your students should *do*: Trust God for protection from demons.

Lesson outline (for the teacher's and students' notebooks):
1. A man controlled by demons (Matthew 8:28; Mark 5:1-5; Luke 8:26-27).
2. Demons recognize Jesus and His power (Matthew 8:29; Mark 5:6-10; Luke 8:28-31).
3. Christ releases the man from demons (Matthew 8:30-33; Mark 5:11-14; Luke 8:32-34).
4. Demons keep people from believing in Jesus (Matthew 8:34; Mark 5:15-21; Luke 8:35-39).

The verse to be memorized:

Submit yourselves therefore to God. Resist the devil, and he will flee from you. (James 4:7)

THE LESSON

1. A MAN CONTROLLED BY DEMONS
Matthew 8:28; Mark 5:1-5; Luke 8:26-27

Show Illustration #1

In the country of the Gadarenes there lived a wild man. He had not always been wild. But one day demons (or evil spirits) came to live in his body. They made him do terrible things he would never have done normally–like tearing off his clothes and cutting himself with sharp stones. Once this man lived in a house. Now he stayed in a cemetery among the tombs, not far from the city of Gadara. The people in the city and in the surrounding country were so afraid of him that they did not even want to pass the place where he was!

At times strong men caught him and bound him with heavy chains and handcuffs. But the demons inside the wild man made him so powerful that he snapped the handcuffs, smashed the chains, broke loose and ran away. No one could tame this man!

Day and night the demons caused the man to scream as he wandered over the wild hills and among the tombs. Often he cut himself with stones. The demons made him do anything they wanted.

2. DEMONS RECOGNIZE JESUS AND HIS POWER
Matthew 8:29; Mark 5:6-10; Luke 8:28-31

Show Illustration #2

It had been a long time since this dangerous man had talked to anyone. But one day he saw men in a boat coming across Lake Galilee. He ran to the shore. When the boat landed, one of the men stepped out. The wild man screamed and fell down before the Stranger. One demon, speaking for the hundreds of demons inside the man, shrieked: "What are you going to do with me, Jesus, Thou Son of the Most High God?"

The man did not know Jesus. But the demons knew Him. They understood He was the Son of God who had far greater power than they did. And they were afraid of Him.

Again the demon spoke: "I beg You, do not torment me yet."

The demons knew that someday they would be eternally punished for their evil ways. But they did not want their punishment to start at this time.

"What is your name?" Jesus asked.

"My name is Legion," the demon answered, for there were many demons inside the man.

Then the demons began to plead with Jesus not to send them to be punished in the prison house of evil spirits (the abyss).

3. CHRIST RELEASES THE MAN FROM DEMONS
Matthew 8:30-33; Mark 5:11-14; Luke 8:32-34

At that moment about 2,000 pigs were feeding on the hillside above Lake Galilee. They were being cared for by some herdsmen. (According to Jewish law, pigs were unclean animals and the Jewish people were not to keep pigs on their land nor eat their meat. These pigs were evidently owned by people who did not obey the law. They probably raised the pigs so they could sell the meat to the Romans for their troops.)

The demons knew about the pigs. So they begged Jesus, "If You cast us out, send us into the pigs."

"Go!" Jesus commanded.

Show Illustration #3

Immediately the demons fled from the man and entered the pigs. Wildly the pigs rushed down the cliff into Lake Galilee where they all drowned.

The herdsmen were terrified. What would the owners of the pigs say? What would the people of the city of Gadara say?

The men dashed to the city shouting: "The pigs are gone! The pigs are gone! They drowned in the lake. Jesus sent the demons out of the wild man into the pigs! They rushed down the mountain into the lake. The pigs are gone!"

4. DEMONS KEEP PEOPLE FROM BELIEVING IN JESUS
Matthew 8:34; Mark 5:15-21; Luke 8:35-39

Show Illustration #4

Immediately great crowds gathered. When they saw the man who had been so full of demons, sitting quietly at the feet of Jesus, they were amazed. The man was dressed. He was in his right mind. The demons were gone. No one would ever again need to fear that man.

Did the people thank Jesus for casting out the demons? No, they did not!

Did they praise God for the wonderful thing that happened that day? No, indeed!

Did they ask Jesus to come into their city so they could learn more about Him and His great power? No!

Instead of being glad, they were frightened. They were afraid, not of the man who had been delivered from the wicked demons, but of the Lord Jesus Christ and His great power. The owners of the pigs, and the people from the city and the surrounding country, cared more about the pigs and the money they would bring than they did about Jesus, the Son of God.

The people begged Jesus to go away and leave them alone. Sadly, the Lord Jesus turned away from the crowd. Satan, the enemy of God, had blinded the minds of the people so they would not know how wonderful Jesus really is. Instead of believing in Him and receiving Him, they rejected Him.

Only one person in all that crowd followed Jesus. That person was the one who had been set free from the demons. As Jesus stepped into the waiting boat, the man begged to go along with Him. He wanted to be with the One who had freed him from the demons.

But Jesus said kindly, "No. Go home to your friends and tell them what great things God has done for you and how He had mercy on you."

As much as the man wanted to be with the Lord Jesus, he willingly obeyed Him. He went to village after village in Decapolis (province) telling the great things God had done for him. People were amazed when they heard about the One who had power over demons.

Surely the man explained that the demons recognized Jesus as the Son of the Most High God. He told how the demons knew they would be sent to eternal punishment. And he certainly told that he himself believed in Jesus, the Son of God. Because he believed in Him, he was forgiven of his sin. Now he would not be separated from God eternally; he would not be punished for his sins.

What else would he have said to all the people in every village? He told them that because the Lord Jesus is all powerful–even more powerful than hundreds of demons–He would forgive their sins if they would believe in Him, God the Son.

And if that man could speak to you today he would ask, "Do you believe in the Lord Jesus Christ as your Saviour? Or have you turned Him away as people did in the long ago?"

If you are a child of God through faith in the Lord Jesus Christ, do not be surprised when Satan attacks you. He has no mercy. Be on guard by knowing God, His Word, and His will. When you obey God, you are submitting yourself to Him (as we are commanded to do in James 4:7). Then, if you refuse to obey the devil, he will go away from you. But like a wild beast, Satan roams about always looking for those he can attack. (See 1 Peter 5:8-9.) All through your life he will tempt you again and again. That is why you must live prayerfully, live carefully. Trust the Lord to help you to look to God for His protection.

God Himself promises: "Fear not; for I am with you: be not dismayed; for I am your God: I will strengthen you; I will help you; I will uphold you with the right hand of My righteousness . . . For I the Lord your God will hold your right hand, saying to you, Fear not: I will help you" (Isaiah 41:10,13). Such assurance from God should make you want to obey Him perfectly.

NOTE TO THE TEACHER

In *Satan the Enemy of God* (New Testament Volume 2), we learned that Satan tried to put an end to the Lord Jesus at His birth, after His baptism, and at His death. But the Son of God triumphed over him. Today Satan and his demons are as real and as vicious as ever. They do not like to be exposed, as you will be exposing them in this series. Be on guard! The command of God to you, teacher, is recorded in Ephesians 6:10-18.

Lesson 2
HEALING A BOY WITH A DEMON

NOTE TO THE TEACHER

In the last lesson we observed that demons are intelligent and wise. They recognized the Lord Jesus Christ as the Son of the Most High God. In this lesson we see that demons have power and they use it for evil, but God is all-powerful.

There is a message for each group in your class: the unbelievers and the believers.

To unbelievers, this is the message: Satan and his host of demons will do their utmost to keep you from turning to the Lord Jesus Christ for forgiveness of sin. But the all-powerful Saviour can dismiss the evil spirits from you. You can be cleansed through faith in the Son of God.

This is the message to those who believe in Christ: The moment you received the Lord Jesus as Saviour, the Holy Spirit of God came to dwell in your heart. He has sealed you as His own possession forever. (See Ephesians 1:13.) Satan and his demons may fiercely tempt you, afflict you, attack you, and influence you. The Word of God warns that the Christian life is a war–a war between the believer and the powers and rulers of darkness. (See Ephesians 6:12.) Our defense against them is the blood of the Lord Jesus Christ and faith in Him. (Study Ephesians 6:10-18; Romans 13:12-14; James 4:7-8.) How is victory assured? By daily walking with the Lord Jesus. That is, by reading the Word of God each day and talking with God in prayer. It is broken fellowship with God and with His Son that opens us to the attack of the enemy of our soul. We must be on guard, walking every moment in the power of the Spirit of God. He is able to keep that which we commit to Him. (See 2 Timothy 1:12.) As we submit ourselves to God and resist Satan, the powers of darkness will flee from us.

To our knowledge, those who have observed demon possession never confuse it with epilepsy. However you may have students who are untaught in these areas. They may conclude that because the boy in the lesson acted in much the same manner as epileptics do, that all who have epilepsy are demon possessed. Nothing could be farther from the truth! Epilepsy is a disease, just as tuberculosis and leprosy are diseases. Diseases are not demon possession. Demons may cause a person to be deaf or mute, to convulse or act in strange ways. But we are wrong to conclude that all such affliction is demon possession. Make certain your students understand this.

Spend time explaining and reviewing the memory verse.

Scripture to be studied: Matthew 17:14-23; Mark 9:14-32; Luke 9:37-45

The *aim* of the lesson: To show that Satan and his demons will try to keep people from believing in Jesus and will tempt and influence Christians.

What your students should *know*: Jesus Christ is Victor over Satan and his hosts of demons.

What your students should *feel*: Confident that Jesus will help those who trust Him.

What your students should *do*:
Saved: Read the Word of God and pray daily so Satan can be defeated when he attacks.
Unsaved: Turn to the Lord Jesus for forgiveness of sin.

Lesson outline (for the teacher's and students' notebooks):
1. The disciples lack power over a demon (Luke 9:37-40).
2. Weak faith cannot overpower demons (Matthew 17:14-17; Mark 9:14-19; Luke 9:37-41).
3. Christ has all power over demons (Matthew 17:18; Mark 9:20-26; Luke 9:42-43).
4. The Lord Jesus gives victory to His own (Matthew 17:19-23; Mark 9:27-29).

The verse to be memorized:

Submit yourselves therefore to God. Resist the devil, and he will flee from you. (James 4:7)

THE LESSON

The 12 disciples of the Lord Jesus had received from Him a power they had never known before. They had His kind of power: power to heal sickness, even the kind of sickness no doctor could cure; power to raise the dead to life; power over demons. (See Luke 9:1; Matthew 10:8.)

The disciples went into the cities and towns with their new power. What a thrill it was for them to see men and women cured of leprosy! The disciples spoke and in a moment the dread disease would leave sick bodies. The disciples even brought dead people back to life through the power of God. They cast out demons in the name of Christ. (See Mark 6:13.) The disciples were so filled with joy that they could hardly wait to tell Jesus of the wonderful things they had done.

1. THE DISCIPLES LACK POWER OVER A DEMON
Luke 9:37-40

But one day something unusual happened. Jesus was away with Peter, James, and John. The other nine disciples were approached by a troubled father who brought his son to them. The boy looked and acted extremely strange. He did not answer when anyone spoke to him.

Show Illustration #5

The father was desperate. "Please heal my son," he begged. "He has a demon in him. Because of the demon he cannot talk, he cannot hear. The demon has done dreadful things to him. Oh, please heal my son!"

The disciples had cast out demons before. Even though Jesus was not with them, the disciples knew He had promised them power for this sort of thing.

The religious leaders and others gathered to watch. Laughing at the disciples they said, "So you can cast out demons, can you? Well, let us see what you can do with this boy. Go ahead! Cast out the demon. Show us your great power."

One of the disciples, doing as he had done before, commanded the demon to come out of the boy. But nothing happened! The people watched and waited. The boy continued to act strangely. He still could not talk. He could not hear. What was wrong? The disciples had never before failed like this. They were embarrassed. Oh, how they wished that Jesus was there!

– 21 –

2. WEAK FAITH CANNOT OVERPOWER DEMONS
Matthew 17:14-17; Mark 9:14-19; Luke 9:37-41

Show Illustration #6

Some of the Jewish leaders threatened the disciples and argued with them. "Why is it you cannot cast out the demon?" they demanded. "We heard that you cast out many demons in other cities. But look! You cannot cast out even one demon from this boy."

In the height of the uproar, someone saw Jesus coming down the mountain with Peter, James, and John. "Look!" he called. "Here comes Jesus!"

Everyone turned from the disciples to the Lord Jesus.

"What were you disputing about?" Jesus asked.

The father of the demon-possessed boy begged Jesus, "Teacher, look at my son, my only son. He cannot talk because he is possessed by a demon. And whenever the demon is in control of him it throws him to the ground. It makes him foam at the mouth, grind his teeth, and become stiff all over. It bruises him and will hardly let go. I brought my boy to Your disciples and begged them to cast out the demon. But they could not."

Jesus turned sadly to the disciples and said, "Oh, what weak faith you have! Bring the boy to Me."

3. CHRIST HAS ALL POWER OVER DEMONS
Matthew 17:18; Mark 9:20-26; Luke 9:42-43

Show Illustration #7

So they brought the boy to Jesus. But when the demon saw Jesus, he made the boy fall to the ground and roll about, foaming at the mouth.

Turning to the father, Jesus asked, "How long has he been like this?"

"Ever since he was a small child," he replied. "Again and again the demon has tried to kill him by throwing him into the fire or into the water. Oh, have pity on us and help us if You can."

"If I can?" Jesus asked. "Everything is possible to the one who believes."

The father cried, "I do believe. Help me to believe more!"

Jesus spoke sharply to the evil spirit. "You dumb and deaf spirit, I command you, come out of him and never go into him again!"

The demon gave a loud scream. The boy trembled fiercely. And the demon came out. The boy lay on the ground without moving. The people standing nearby exclaimed, "He is dead!"

4. THE LORD JESUS GIVES VICTORY TO HIS OWN
Matthew 17:19-23; Mark 9:27-29

Show Illustration #8

But Jesus tenderly took him by the hand. The boy stood to his feet, alive and perfectly well! He could speak. He could hear.

The people returned to their homes, astonished at the power of God. Did they believe in the Lord Jesus Christ? We do not know. Some of them may have.

The disciples had seen the power of God at work once again. But they were troubled. When at last they were alone with the Lord they asked Him, "Why could we not cast out the demon?"

"Because of your little faith," Jesus told them. "Nothing will be impossible to you, if you have faith enough. This kind of demon can come out only through faith and prayer."

Now the disciples realized that it was their own fault that the demon had not obeyed them. They had not prayed in real faith, resting in the power of God alone. Perhaps they had become proud of all they had accomplished before, unconsciously believing they had some power in themselves.

The disciples had no power over the demon apart from the power of God and prayer. Just so, you and I can have no power over Satan and his demons without the power of God and believing prayer. Satan and his demons are strong, wise, cunning–stronger and wiser than we are. But the Lord Jesus Christ is Victor over Satan and his hosts of demons.

NOTE TO THE TEACHER

Satan and his army of demons are constantly warring against you and your students.

The demon controlled the boy in our lesson. And Satan and his demons control those in your class who are not born again. The demon kept the boy from hearing. And Satan blinds the mind of the unbeliever (2 Corinthians 4:4) so he does not hear the good news of salvation–even though he may seem to be listening as you teach. Or, if he does hear the message, Satan aims to snatch the Word from his heart so he will not believe and be saved (Luke 8:12).

The unbeliever can be loosed from the grip of Satan if you yourself are controlled by the Spirit of God. Your careful teaching must be accompanied with prayerful preparation. And your lesson must be given in the power of the Holy Spirit.

The members of your class who are believers in the Lord Jesus Christ, are also being warred upon by Satan and his demons. Perhaps this very day some are being tempted to lie. (See Acts 5:3.) Some may be tempted to do that which is immoral. (See 1 Corinthians 7:5.) Others may be defeated today. Satan uses his demons to do this. (See Ephesians 6:11-12.) Some of your students may be persecuted for their faith in Christ. (See Revelation 2:10.) Some may have been falsely accused. (See Revelation 12:10.) Yet others may be hindered in their purpose to do the will of God. (See 1 Thessalonians 2:18.) Many may be proud. (Proverbs 16:5; 1 Peter 5:5.) These attacks of the devil are very, very real. Seek to meet the immediate needs of each member of your class, Teacher!

Lesson 3
JESUS CASTS OUT A DEMON AND IS ACCUSED

NOTE TO THE TEACHER

In this lesson, Satan and his demons are seen at work in the demon-possessed man and also in the minds of the people in the crowd. Satan works in obvious ways and also in subtle, deceptive ways.

In the past two lessons you have taught that demons are clever and powerful, but that they are not all-wise and all-powerful as God is. You understand that demons are free to tempt even the believing child of God. They may afflict the believer, attack him, influence him.

When the Lord Jesus Christ gave His precious blood on the cross of Calvary and then rose from the dead, Satan was defeated. Satan knows this. But he, the ruler of darkness, continues his war against believers. The believer is victorious over the awful attacks of Satan and his demons by having a daily walk with the Son of God, reading the Word of God faithfully, and by earnest prayer.

In this lesson you should take time to explain that demons are continually active in many places. But they are not everywhere present at the same time, as God is. We cannot stop Satan and his demons from going where they want to on the earth. But God–who is higher and greater than Satan and the demons–can stop them.

If you have careless believers in your class–those who are not walking in fellowship with the Lord Jesus and in His strength–warn them that they are open to the attacks of the evil one. If you have those who are overcome with fear, give them the assurance that, when they are having a daily walk with Christ, He keeps them safe. He is all-powerful!

Scripture to be studied: Matthew 12:22-45; Mark 3:22-30; Luke 11:14-28

The *aim* of the lesson: To show that while demons are active in many places, they are not present everywhere as God is.

What your students should *know*: Satan cannot reign over one in whose life the Lord Jesus reigns.

What your students should *feel*: Assurance that Jesus will help overcome Satan's temptations.

What your students should *do*: Have a daily walk with God by reading His Word and praying.

Lesson outline (for the teacher's and students' notebooks):

1. The demon cast out by Jesus (Matthew 12:22-28; Mark 3:22-26; Luke 11:14-20).
2. Christians need the protection of Someone stronger than Satan (Matthew 12:29-45; Mark 3:27-30; Luke 11:21-26).
3. Jesus protects His own because He is stronger than Satan (Luke 11:27-28).
4. We can defeat Satan with the Word of God and prayer (Ephesians 6:10, 17-18).

The verse to be learned:

Submit yourselves therefore to God. Resist the devil, and he will flee from you. (James 4:7)

THE LESSON

1. THE DEMON CAST OUT BY JESUS
Matthew 12:22-28; Mark 3:22-26; Luke 11:14-20

One day many crowded around the Lord Jesus. These people had heard strange stories about this One who explained that He is the Son of God. They heard that He made the blind to see, the deaf to hear, the crippled to walk. Even more amazing, it was said that Jesus could command demons to come out of people. Was it really true? Could Jesus do all these mighty acts? The people were determined to find out for themselves.

As they watched and waited, a man was brought to Jesus. The man could walk. But he could not see. Nor could he talk. A demon had entered his body. (It should be remembered that not all physical affliction is due to demons, though in this case, it was.)

Could Jesus do anything for such a man? Would He be able to cast out the demon and make the man speak again?

Show Illustration #9

The Bible does not record exactly what the Lord Jesus said to the man. But it does say that Jesus cast out the demon. The people were astonished when the man began to speak. He was healed! The demon really was gone!

"How did Jesus do it?" "How did He make the demon leave the man?" These were among the questions the people asked each other as they looked at Jesus and the man whom He had healed. No one could deny the fact that the Lord Jesus had cast out the demon. Everyone had seen Him do it. But how did He do it?

"I know!" someone said. "He has Beelzebub and by the chief of demons he casts out demons."

What or who was Beelzebub? It was the Fly-god–the god who was supposed to have power to protect people from harmful insects. The Jews, who hated such false gods, changed the name to Filth-god (because flies were known to live on refuse). To show their complete hatred for this make-believe god, they applied the name to Satan.

And now they let it be known that they felt that the Lord Jesus Christ–the One who went about doing good–received His power from Satan. Oh, what a dreadful thing to say!

He, God the Son, could have struck them dead for speaking so irreverently. But He knew that Satan had made them blind to the truth that He is the Son of God. So, instead of putting them to death, he sought to teach them. He did so by asking a question and immediately giving them three answers to that question.

He asked, "How can Satan cast out Satan?" If it had been Satan who cast out the demon, then he had cast out part of his own army. Would Satan cast out part of himself?

First, Jesus said, "When a country (kingdom) divides itself into groups which fight against each other, that country will not last very long." The people could understand this.

Second, the Lord Jesus continued, "When members of a family (house) fight one another and have arguments, that family will fall apart." Again the people knew what Jesus meant.

Third, the Lord Jesus explained, "If what you have been saying about Me is true–that Satan is giving Me power to cast out his demons–then he is fighting against himself. How can his kingdom last?" Satan was the one who sent the demons to possess the people, hurt them, and make them do evil things. Surely, therefore, he would not want to have his demons cast out of people.

2. CHRISTIANS NEED THE PROTECTION OF SOMEONE STRONGER THAN SATAN
Matthew 12:29-45; Mark 3:27-30; Luke 11:21-26

Show Illustration #10

Those who listened knew that what Jesus said was true. They could not argue with Him. But Jesus had not finished speaking. He continued: "When a strong man arms himself and carefully guards his palace, everything he owns is safe. But if someone stronger than he attacks the palace, he is defeated. The stronger man takes away the armor of the weaker man and divides all his goods."

The Lord Jesus wanted the people to see that Satan was like the man in the palace and that only someone stronger than Satan could attack and defeat him. Who is stronger than Satan? God! He can overcome Satan and all his demons.

Jesus, God the Son, had more to say about demons. "When a demon is cast out of a man," He explained, "he goes to the desert looking for a place to rest. When he does not find any, he says, 'I will go back to the house–the body–which I just left.' So he goes back and finds the house (body) clean and all in order. Then he goes out again and gets seven other demons more evil than himself and they all enter the person and live in the same body. And so the individual is worse off than he was at the beginning."

3. JESUS PROTECTS HIS OWN BECAUSE HE IS STRONGER THAN SATAN
Luke 11:27-28

Jesus was warning the man who had been delivered from the demon, as well as all who listened. He was explaining that

it is not enough simply to have the demon cast out. Demons can reenter a person. The man needed Someone stronger than the demons to come and live in his life. Who is stronger than Satan and his demons? God is stronger.

Show Illustration #11

When we receive His beloved Son as our Saviour, inviting Him into our hearts and lives, He can–and will–protect us.

One woman in the crowd had been listening carefully. Realizing how wonderful Jesus is, she exclaimed, "Blessed be Your mother for having such a Son!"

The Lord Jesus knew what the woman meant. Kindly He answered her, speaking for all to hear, "But even more blessed are those who hear the Word of God and obey it."

The people had heard the Word of God from the lips of the Son of God. But would they believe and obey Him? Would they believe in the Lord Jesus as their Saviour? Would they let Him be their protection against Satan and his demons?

4. WE CAN DEFEAT SATAN WITH THE WORD OF GOD AND PRAYER
Ephesians 6:10, 17-18

Everyone who listened to the Lord Jesus that day had to make a choice. We do not know what choice they made.

But today you, too, have a choice to make. You may be trying to keep your life clean and pure by your own strength. Perhaps you say, "No demon will ever influence my life." But remember, you are not strong enough in yourself. You need One who is stronger than you are–One who is stronger than Satan and all his demons. That One is the Lord Jesus Christ. When you place your trust in Him, you become His property. Then, as you yield yourself to Him, you have His strength to resist Satan.

Show Illustration #12

Satan will not stop tempting you. He will attack you with his awful power. The Lord Jesus Himself was tested by Satan. How did He meet that testing? Each time He answered Satan by quoting the Word of God. If, for example, Satan and his demons put into your mind an unclean thought, say, "God says, 'Be ye holy; for I am holy'." (1 Peter 1:16). If Satan causes you to doubt your salvation, say, "God says, 'He who has the Son has life; and he who has not the Son of God has not life' " (1 John 5:12).

Continually talk with God, thanking Him for the Lord Jesus Christ who gave His precious blood so you can have eternal life. Yield yourself to God. Willingly obey Him. Allow the Lord Jesus to reign as King of your life. Resist Satan through the power of God. Then he will flee from you.

Whenever you feel afraid of Satan and his demons, remember this wonderful truth: "You are of God, little children, and have overcome them; because greater is He that is in you, than he that is in the world" (1 John 4:4).

> **NOTE TO THE TEACHER**
> Make it perfectly clear to your students that demons cannot reign over anyone in whose heart Jesus Christ reigns. In resisting the devil, we may–and must–count on the protection of the Lord Jesus Christ.

Lesson 4
DEMONS

> **NOTE TO THE TEACHER**
>
> In this series of lessons we have seen how vicious can be the attacks of Satan and his demons. You may live in a land where you have seen unbelievers possessed of demons. You may have seen believers attacked and afflicted by demons. You have seen with your own eyes to what extremes Satan will go to hold on to one of his subjects, or to attack one of his former subjects. You know the horror of such experiences.
>
> If, however, you live in a land where you have not seen such events as recorded in these lessons, you may find it a bit more difficult to teach them. Indeed, you may be strongly tempted (and that by the devil himself!) not to teach them at all. Do not yield to the wiles of the evil one. Help your students to see that Satan sometimes appears as an angel of light (2 Corinthians 11:14). His first thrust on earth was simply a question to Eve: "Has God said?" Causing us to doubt God and His Word may not be as dramatic as being possessed or attacked by demons. But the consequences are equally grim.
>
> "Wherewithal shall a young man cleanse his way? by taking heed thereto according to Thy Word . . . Thy Word have I hid in mine heart, that I might not sin against Thee" (Psalm 119:9, 11).
>
> Keep your heart and mind centered upon God. Give yourself wholly to Him. Resist the devil and he will flee from you. The Word of God says so. And the Word of God is true!

The aim of the lesson: To show that although demons are powerful now, they will one day be destroyed forever.

What your students should *know*: The attacks of Satan and his demons are real and fierce.

What your students should *feel*: A keen desire to submit to God and His Word.

What your students should *do*: Allow the Lord Jesus to control their lives.

Lesson outline (for the teacher's and students' notebooks):

1. Demons are powerful, wicked, unclean spirits (Luke 11:24-26).
2. Demons try to keep people from believing the Word of God and trusting in Jesus (Luke 8:26-28; Ephesians 6:12).
3. We are protected from demons by submitting to God and His Word (1 John 4:4; Ephesians 6:10-18).
4. Demons will be cast into the Lake of Fire forever (Matthew 25:41; Revelation 20:10).

The verse to be memorized:

Submit yourselves therefore to God. Resist the devil, and he will flee from you. (James 4:7)

THE LESSON

Sometime ago we studied about a beautiful angel named Lucifer. Do you remember what his name meant? It meant Son of the Morning. He was important because God had chosen him to rule over many angels. But one day this beautiful angel had a wicked, selfish thought. He wanted to be as high and as great as God. That was sin. Lucifer was not perfect any more. So God took away his high position. No longer could he rule over the other angels. No longer could he be called Lucifer, the Son of the Morning. His name was changed to Satan or the Devil.

Ever since then Satan has been the enemy of God. With him are demons—a great army of them—who help the devil in his evil work. In the last three lessons we learned that Satan's demons are wise and powerful. They go throughout the entire earth working against God. Today we will learn more about Satan and his army of demons so we can know how to stand against them.

We are not exactly certain where these demons came from. But we do know that there are uncounted numbers of them. One of the men of whom we studied in these lessons was possessed by hundreds of demons.

Demons are the helpers of the devil. Not only do they want to destroy the work and plan of God but they want to build up the work of Satan, "the god of this world." (See 2 Corinthians 4:4.)

1. DEMONS ARE POWERFUL, WICKED, UNCLEAN SPIRITS
Luke 11:24-26

Show Illustration #13

1. Demons are powerful spirits without human bodies. They do have some kind of body which is invisible to us. They are real beings which think, move, see, and speak. They are very wise. They know more than human beings know. But they are not all-wise or all-powerful as God is. Surprisingly, they know that Jesus is the Son of God. (See James 2:19.) In our first lesson, you will remember that the demon cried, "What are You going to do with me Jesus, Son of the Most High God? I beg You, do not torment me yet."

2. Demons are wicked. Sometimes the Word of God calls them unclean spirits. (See Luke 9:42; 11:24.) That is why they caused the boy (in our second lesson) to throw himself into the fire or the water. If they cannot accomplish their purposes by doing evil things, they will make evil things look as if they are good and right. (See 2 Corinthians 11:14-15.) (In our illustration, the one in front represents the "angel of light.")

3. Demons enter the bodies of unbelievers and take control of them. They can make them blind, or deaf, or dumb. Often they make them do wild, terrible things. (Teacher: Review briefly the people mentioned in the first three lessons. However, be certain that the class understands that not all who are blind, deaf, or cannot speak, are possessed with demons.)

4. Because demons are enemies of all who believe in the Lord Jesus Christ as Saviour, they constantly war against Christians. (See Ephesians 6:10-18.) They try to get them to disobey the Lord Jesus and obey Satan.

2. DEMONS TRY TO KEEP PEOPLE FROM BELIEVING THE WORD OF GOD AND TRUSTING IN JESUS
Luke 8:26-28; Ephesians 6:12

Show Illustration #14

1. Demons try to keep everyone everywhere from believing the Word of God and from trusting that the Lord Jesus Christ is the Son of God. They themselves know who Jesus is, but they do not want anyone on earth to believe He died and rose again. They do not want people to trust the Lord Jesus and become His child by receiving Him.

2. Demons try to cause those who have trusted in the Lord Jesus and received Him as Saviour, to be disobedient to God. They do not want the children of God to read the Word of God. They do not want God's children to pray to Him. They want believers in Christ to go their own way instead of in the way of God.

3. WE ARE PROTECTED FROM DEMONS BY SUBMITTING TO GOD AND HIS WORD
1 John 4:4; Ephesians 6:10-18

Show Illustration #15

1. The greatest protection against demons is to have the Lord Jesus Christ living in your heart and life. We have this assurance: "greater is He that is in you, than he that is in the world" (1 John 4:4; see also Ephesians 1:19; Colossians 2:15; 1 John 3:8.).

2. Because the Christian life is a war against Satan and his awful army of demons,

we mus submit ourselves willfully and obediently to God. He will help us to do this as we read His Word and obey it. By taking time to memorize certain verses, we can use them against Satan when he tempts us to do wrong. The Word of God is called "the sword of the Spirit." (See Ephesians 6:10-18.) That "sword," quoted to Satan, makes him flee. It is important to have set times of prayer–times when we talk to God alone. But at any time, in any place, we can cry to God for help in fighting the powers of Satan and his demons. God is always ready to help us.

DEMONS WILL BE CAST INTO THE LAKE OF FIRE FOREVER
Matthew 25:41; Revelation 20:10

Show Illustration #16

One day Satan and all his demons will be cast into the Lake of Fire forever and forever. (Read Matthew 25:41; Revelation 20:10.) In that day, Jesus, the King of kings and Lord of lords, will reign. Now, if the Lord Jesus reigns in your heart, Satan and his demons are as powerless as they will be in the Lake of Fire. The Lord Jesus will reign in your heart if you submit yourself to Him, trusting Him to control your life. Will you yield to Him now?

A NOTE TO THE TEACHER

The purpose of this study has been (1) to make us aware of the wiles of Satan and his demons; and (2) to prepare us to stand against the attacks of the enemy.

God has made ample provision for every Christian. With Christ Jesus we can overcome Satan and his demons. (See Revelation 12:11.) The Lord Jesus has given us the victory. We must claim that victory by faith, submitting to God and resisting Satan and his demons.

Have you wondered what is the exact meaning of submitting yourself to God? To submit to God is to allow Him to take control.

One who lives in Africa had long been demon possessed. Now she is a believer in Christ Jesus the Lord. She told others in her village, "You know, my sisters, sometimes the demons come to attack me and I fear them. Then in my helplessness I just say, 'Jesus, Jesus,' and I repeat that wonderful name over and over again until the demons disappear. They do not like to hear that wonderful name–Jesus." She willingly allows the Lord Jesus to control her life.

God has made all of us with wills of our own. We can choose to live in obedience to Him, walk with Him, talk with Him, and read His Word. We can memorize His Word and use it when Satan attacks us. Even though we are children of God by faith in Christ Jesus, we can choose to do our own will instead of the will of God. But if we go our own way, disobeying God and sinning willfully, we are open to all the awful attacks of Satan and his demons. However, God is faithful. (See 1 Corinthians 10:13 and 2 Timothy 2:13.) He knows those who are His. (See 2 Timothy 2:19.) So, as we confidently trust Him, He enables us to resist the devil, the fearsome enemy of our souls.

www.ingramcontent.com/pod-product-compliance
Lightning Source LLC
Chambersburg PA
CBHW060805090426
42736CB00002B/161